Juv.
R

# Tools for Writing

D1059236

CORWIN
PRESS

**The Corwin Press logo**—a raven striding across an open book—represents the happy union of courage and learning. We are a professional-level publisher of books and journals for K–12 educators, and we are committed to creating and providing resources that embody these qualities. Corwin's motto is "Success for All Learners."

# Tools for Writing

## Creating Writer's Workshops for Grades 2-8

Barbara Z. Boone

**CORWIN PRESS, INC.**
A Sage Publications Company
Thousand Oaks, California

*For information address:*

Corwin Press, Inc.
A Sage Publications Company
2455 Teller Road
Thousand Oaks, California 91320
e-mail: order@corwin.sagepub.com

SAGE Publications Ltd.
6 Bonhill Street
London EC2A 4PU
United Kingdom

SAGE Publications India Pvt. Ltd.
M-32 Market
Greater Kailash I
New Delhi 110 048 India

Printed in the United States of America

**Library of Congress Cataloging-in-Publication Data**

Boone, Barbara Z.
    Tools for writing : creating writer's workshops for grades 2-8 /
Barbara Z. Boone.
        p.   cm.
    Includes bibliographical references (p. 118-126).
    ISBN 0-8039-6456-0 (c : alk. paper). — ISBN 0-8039-6457-9 (p :
alk. paper)
    1. English language—Composition and exercises—Study and teaching
(Elementary)—United States. 2. Creative writing—Study and
teaching (Elementary)—United States.   I. Title.
LB1576.B5248   1996
372.6'23—dc20                                              96-16600

This book is printed on acid-free paper.

96  97  98  99  00  10  9  8  7  6  5  4  3  2  1

Corwin Press Production Editor: S. Marlene Head

# Contents

## 3. The Craft of Writing: Minilessons     62

# Foreword

From my vantage point in the National Writing Project, I look out across the country and see how rich, diverse, and widespread is the movement we have come to call writer's workshop. Grounded in a set of deep beliefs about young people and their capacities as authors, proponents of writer's workshop challenge us to rethink many aspects of the conventional wisdom of school: how we spend our time together in school, how we should relate to each other in the classroom community, what we should learn while we are learning writing. And somehow, all the pieces fit together in such a way that it does not seem possible to rethink one piece without eventually making one's way to the others. We should be generous with ourselves—the task is daunting.

For several years now, I have had the privilege of watching Barbara Boone make her own way through the process of becoming a workshop teacher. I have also been privileged to watch as she opened up her practice—her experimentations, successes, and challenges—to other teachers. Her sense of what would be useful, of what colleagues might share as they put together the puzzle pieces of their new approach, has made her a valued workshop leader, mentor, and colleague. In many of her teacher workshops, she encountered colleagues who were encouraged to take their first steps toward writer's workshop because she presented her first steps with clarity and precision. She understood that few of us are willing to embark on what seem to be impossible tasks.

It was her sense of what might useful, when and to whom, that was the birth of this book. Starting as a simple idea bank that could be shared in workshops and around faculty room tables, it grew and grew. Colleagues asked for more and contributed their own ideas. Teachers in inservice courses shaped it. Most importantly, students shaped it.

The result is something handy, something dandy—to coin a phrase. Like a favorite cookbook, *Tools for Writing: Creating Writer's Workshops for Grades 2-8* is meant to be consulted, to spark ideas, to invite creative substitutions and routine adaptations. It also invites additions, recipes for new dishes scribbled on kitchen cards tucked between the pages. Most of all, it invites shoptalk. I am sure you'll be happy to have it on your shelf.

ELYSE EIDMAN-AADAHL
*Associate Director*
*National Writing Project*

# Preface

I implemented a writer's workshop approach to teaching writing in my classroom in the 1990 school year after taking an inservice course offered by my school district. That approach changed my ideas about writing and the teaching of writing forever. I learned about the process approach to writing that included prewriting, drafting, revising, and editing. Not only did those processes help me tremendously in my personal writing, but they also helped me to understand how to teach children to write. Never have I had students who were so eager to write and share their writing as I did when I used the workshop technique. Because of their enthusiasm, I was eager to teach writing for the first time in my career.

In the summer of 1991, after attending an institute on writing at Towson State University in Towson, Maryland, I became a teacher-consultant for the Maryland Writing Project. The presentation I developed for that institute showed teachers how to set up a writer's workshop in their classrooms. During the next 5 years, I made presentations to teachers throughout the state of Maryland helping them to implement the workshop approach in their classrooms. It became clear, as I continued to implement the writing workshop in my classroom and give presentations, that there were very few resources available for teachers to create minilessons for the workshop approach. Minilessons make up the heart of the workshop. There were excellent books that discussed how to teach writing and use the workshop approach, but none that were specifically written about minilessons for writer's workshop in a step-by-step, concise way. I had to wade through a lot of narrative material in most of the writing books before I could find an idea for a minilesson. When I first set up the workshop, I spent many hours deciding what to teach in the minilessons and looking for resources that had ideas for those lessons. I later developed another presentation for the Maryland Writing Project to share ideas for minilessons with teachers. I remember saying during one presentation that maybe I should write a book of minilessons for writer's workshop. Well, here I am, writing that book.

This book is a collection of 72 minilessons for writer's workshop that will give teachers in Grades 2 through 8 procedures for setting up a workshop in their classrooms, forms to use, ideas to generate topics for writing, and skill lessons on the craft of writing. The lessons have been compiled over a period of 5 years working with writer's workshop in a fourth-grade classroom. Each year, the lessons were adapted to the group of students, allowing for different interests and ability levels. Some lessons remained constant, whereas others were fine-tuned as I gathered more information about the writing process with my students. Most of the lessons are generic in nature so that teachers of Grades 2 through 8 can adapt them to their level by using appropriate reading material for the lessons.

The book's purpose is to provide busy teachers with quick access to many lesson ideas that do not require lots of materials to implement in a format that is easy to follow. It is divided into three main sections. Chapter 1, Getting Started: Procedural Minilessons, provides minilessons on procedures to set up writer's workshop in the classroom. It begins by introducing the three components of writer's workshop (minilesson, writing time, celebration) and ends with suggestions for yearly planning. These lessons will establish routines in the classroom for using materials and forms and responding to writing. These first lessons will provide teachers new to the workshop approach with a starting point. Please consult the bibliography for other resources if you need more detailed information on setting up writer's workshop. The book will briefly mention writing time and celebration, which are the other two components of the workshop. However, the focus is on minilessons.

All writers, especially beginning ones, need topics to write about. Teachers need to motivate students with ideas for writing. Chapter 2 provides topic-choice minilessons that will stimulate students to think of ideas for writing. Teachers should choose several topic-choice lessons at the beginning of every semester to reinvigorate students with new ideas.

Chapter 3, The Craft of Writing: Minilessons, provides lessons that will help teachers teach children the craft of fiction writing. Teachers have been teaching these kinds of lessons for years in their language arts classrooms. These are the skills that students need to learn to become more effective story writers, and they were the hardest ones for me to find or create in a concise manner on a teacher's busy schedule. I hope that I have saved teachers much research time. I have included lessons in the beginning that will help students build a foundation of words to use in their writing. Teachers can elaborate on these lessons. I recommend that teachers begin fiction writing by doing lots of modeling and class stories before students attempt to write stories on their own. I have not included any lessons on the mechanics of writing because I know that teachers can incorporate their grammar lessons from the past into their workshop lessons. Teachers should also be using curriculum from their school districts, their students' writing, and their own writing for other ideas for minilessons.

The Appendix at the end of the book includes forms to evaluate the workshop, keep track of conferences, and summarize each semester. Many of these forms will be useful for reporting students' progress to parents and for use on report cards.

Each lesson is created on a clipboard so that it can be read quickly and implemented with a minimum number of materials. Where specific books are suggested, teachers may feel free to substitute others that are equally appropriate and still maintain the lesson idea.

# Acknowledgments

I would like to thank the Maryland Writing Project, and especially the class of 1991, for providing me with my first taste of what it means to become a writer. The minigrant that I received from the MWP allowed me to pilot the book during the 1994-1995 school year. A special thanks to Dr. Elyse Eidman-Aadahl, Director of the National Writing Project, for being my adviser on the project and for agreeing to write the foreword for the book.

I would like to acknowledge the teachers who piloted the minilessons for me last year and gave me feedback on them. Thanks to Mt. Airy Elementary School in Mt. Airy, Maryland: Susan Meyer, Hether Shulman, Ann Marie Blonkowski, Donna Beeman, Patti Cannaday, Patricia McGee, Rispa Arnett, Eileen Haight, and Phyllis Sonnenleiter. Thanks to Villa Cresta Elementary School in Baltimore, Maryland: Jackie Dutton, Barbara Lipp, Laura Lagomarsino, Carolyn Foster, Betty Riley, Barbara Yingling, Colleen Fallano, Marie Erline. Thanks to Hampton Elementary School in Lutherville, Maryland: Carol Whiteford, and Winfield Elementary School in Baltimore, Maryland: Eunice Hopper. Thanks to Betty Riley, Colleen Fallano, Barbara Yingling, Betty Kansler, and Maggie Madden for reviewing the book for publication.

Thanks to the teachers throughout the state of Maryland who attended the inservice courses where I gave my presentation for their enthusiastic reception of my ideas. Thanks to Deborah Fitzell for her help in editing the book and to Alison Donlon and family members for their words of encouragement. Without the students in my classes for the last 5 years, I would not have been able to try my ideas for these minilessons. Thanks to the students at Villa Cresta Elementary in Baltimore, Maryland and their parents for their words of encouragement my last year there.

I am especially proud to have completed the Master's in Professional Writing at Towson State University in Towson, Maryland. I am grateful to the professors in that writing program. Thanks to my adviser, Dr. Sharon Gibson, and a special thanks to Helen Jean Burn for making me believe that I could write and for all of her advice in getting this book published.

My final, but not least important, acknowledgment goes to God for guiding me on this wonderful journey the last 5 years.

BARBARA Z. BOONE
*Baltimore, Maryland*

# About the Author

I was born and raised in Baltimore, Maryland. I earned a B.A. in elementary education in 1969 and an M.S. in professional writing in 1995 from Towson State University in Baltimore, and an M.S. in elementary education from Morgan State University, also in Baltimore, in 1977.

My teaching career spanned 25 years in Grades 2 through 5 in the Baltimore County Public School System. I spent many summers writing curriculum for the county schools and teaching inservice courses to county teachers.

My love for writing began with an inservice writing course that I took in 1990. I implemented a writer's workshop in my classroom that year. At that point, the writing seed was planted. The following summer, I took the summer institute offered by the Maryland Writing Project and became a teacher-consultant for the MWP. I have given workshops to teachers throughout the state of Maryland for the past 5 years, showing teachers how to set up a writer's workshop in their classrooms. Although I have retired from classroom teaching, I continue to do presentations and teach inservice courses on writer's workshop. This book grew out of those presentations.

I continue to work on writing projects on a volunteer basis as I search for a new career that will combine my education with my writing skills.

# Introduction

The writer's workshop approach to teaching writing became popular in the 1980s with experts such as Lucy Calkins, Nancie Atwell, Donald Murray, Donald Graves, Mary Ellen Giacobbe, Susan Sowers, and others who studied how writers and children go about the task of writing. They found that writers need three things to be effective: time to write, ownership of their writing, and response to their writing (Atwell, 1987).

Writers need time that is regularly scheduled every day. Many language arts classrooms did not and many today still do not schedule regular time for their students to write. Scheduled time for writing allows students to build habits that contribute to becoming good writers. It allows them to use the processes of writing that professional writers use: prewriting, drafting, revising, and editing. To accomplish all of this, writers need more time to write than we are used to giving them. By setting up a writing workshop in the classroom, students are guaranteed the first essential for writers—regular writing time. Donald Graves suggests giving students at least three class periods a week for writing (Atwell, 1987). I gave students three and sometimes four class periods of 1 hour each per week for writing. This did not include other writing that we did in the classroom, such as journal writing or content writing in other subjects.

Writers need to have writing materials at their disposal: paper, pencils, dictionaries, staplers, tape, folders for storing work, markers, paper clips, a thesaurus. Teachers who use the workshop approach set up a special spot in the classroom just for these supplies. Students know exactly where to go when they need supplies and how to use them for their writing. This predictable structure gives students a sense of ownership of the writing workshop—the second essential for writers (Atwell, 1987). The sense of ownership extends to the topics that they write about. A writing workshop allows students to choose their own topics. This is not to say that a teacher can never assign or suggest a topic. In fact, it is the teacher's responsibility to provide motivation from time to time for ideas on what to write about. When students choose what they write about it gives them an investment in their own writing. The first year that I set up the workshop in my classroom, I was very skeptical and afraid to give students the freedom to choose their own topics. But what I discovered was the opposite of what I feared. After hearing some motivational ideas from me, they did not have trouble thinking of things to write about. They were eager to write and willing to share what they had written. This had not been my previous experience with students and writing, but I found that once you have turned students on to something (like writing), there is no stopping them. I am speaking of students at all levels of ability, even those with limited writing skills.

The third component that writers need for their work is response to their writing. I never understood this until I began working on a degree in writing. In the classes I attended, students would sit around in a circle, listen as each other's writing was read aloud, and then respond to it. What a scary experience at first, but so valuable. This was the first time that I had let anyone but the teacher look at what I wrote. I had a hard time understanding that others sometimes could not comprehend what I meant when I wrote something. Listening to their responses and questions about my work made the revising process so much easier. I had a direction for my revisions. I now understand what the experts mean by response to writing and can see the benefits for my students as well. The writing workshop approach allows for a response time for writers. However, teachers need to guide and model appropriate responding for students. As Nancie Atwell (1987) says: "A writer wants response that takes the writer seriously and moves him or her forward, again, response that gives help without threatening the writer's dignity" (p. 66). Time, ownership, and response—essentials for writers.

Writer's workshop, which is a way of organizing classroom writing instruction, allows for the essentials through its three components: the minilesson, writing time, and celebration. The first of the three components, the minilesson, is the heart of this book. I will describe this component in detail. The other two components will be outlined, but further exploration may be needed for those teachers who have never used the workshop approach. Suggested references are in the Bibliography. The minilesson is a short (10 to 15 minutes) teacher-directed lesson given at the beginning of the workshop time for the whole class or a small group of students. It teaches a very specific skill or shows students a procedure used in the workshop. The procedural lessons are used to set up the workshop in the classroom. Each teacher must set up procedures for the workshop that are comfortable for the teacher and the students. Once these procedures are in place, the teacher can focus on topic-choice minilessons to motivate students to write and later craft writing lessons that teach specific writing skills. Ideas for minilessons may come from the curriculum required by school districts, students' writing needs as evidenced through their writing, the teacher's writing, and other writing sources such as this book. I found it helpful to make a visual for the classroom for each minilesson and post it somewhere in the classroom where students could be reminded of previous minilessons.

The second component of the writer's workshop is writing time during which students write on topics of their own choice developed from topic lists or through minilessons. Writing time usually lasts from 15 to 20 minutes and follows the minilesson. During this time, many activities may be taking place in the classroom. Students will be moving through different stages as they write: prewriting, drafting, revising, and editing. They may have conferences with the teacher or with peers to get response to their writing at any stage. They need not wait until a piece is completed before they share their writing. In fact, it is more beneficial to get response before the final draft. The teacher will be walking around the room, stopping at children's desks to discuss their writing, or having individual conferences at a designated spot in the room.

The third component of the writer's workshop is celebration in which students share their writing for feedback from their peers. It lasts from 15 to 20 minutes and follows the writing time. I always used celebration with the entire class. Some teachers use it with small groups. Students respond to each other's writing through a process called praise, question, polish (PQP). One student volunteers to read a piece of writing to the group. After hearing the piece, the rest of the students give the writer *praise* for his or her writing. Following praise, students ask the writer *questions* about the writing; something that is not clear, perhaps. After the questions, the class gives the writer suggestions to improve (*polish*) the writing. I limited the praise, questions, and polish to three of each for the sake of time. I wrote or had a student write the questions and polish on a form (see Figure 1.5) that the writer attached to his or her writing for use during revision. Teachers must come up with their own system for deciding who will read their writing each day. I put the students' names on clothespins, which were put on the edge of a basket. One child would pick a name off of the edge of the basket. That child could decide to read that day or pass one time only. If his or her piece was read that day, then the clothespin went into the basket until all of the other students had a turn. After all students had had a turn sharing, all clothespins were put on the edge of the basket for a new round of sharing. For most celebrations, I had two or three students share their writing.

# 1

## Getting Started:
## Procedural Minilessons

*Procedural Minilessons for Writer's Workshop*

This section will describe how to set up a writer's workshop in the elementary classroom. Except for the first two, the lessons do not have to be followed in sequence. Praise, question, polish should be introduced in that order, but the teacher may introduce the concept of celebration whenever it is appropriate. I would suggest introducing all of the lessons in this section in order to get the workshop up and running. Each idea should be used for one minilesson. If a lesson takes more than 10 to 15 minutes, continue it in the next session of the workshop. Writing time and celebration should follow the minilesson, even if all of the procedures have not yet been introduced. Students can begin to write before all of the components to the workshop have been established. It is important that they write every day. By writing every session, students will build up a collection of writing that can be used for future minilessons and pieces that can be revisited in another session of the workshop. All writing should be kept in writing folders in the classroom so that students have access to them every day.

### Introducing the Three Components
### of Writer's Workshop

1. Tell students that writer's workshop consists of three parts: minilesson (teacher's time for lesson on writing), writing time (students' time for writing), and celebration (sharing of writing).

2. Brainstorm the meaning of the word *writing*. Ask students what they like to write about.

3. Discuss what it means to be an author.

## Starting a Topic List

Use one of the following ideas to start a list of topics for students to use for writing. Have them keep the list in their writing folders. Add to the list through other lessons.

1. Make a web of ideas for writing by giving students words to use in the web; for example, interests, people, places. Refer to the next chapter for more specific details.

2. Brainstorm with the class topics that students enjoy writing about. Make a copy of the topics for each student.

3. Get ideas from books in the classroom and put them on the list.

4. Use one of the ideas from the chapter on topic-choice minilessons.

### Introducing the Praise Technique for Celebration

1. Praise several students for something they have done.

2. Ask them to name a word that tells what you just did (praise).

3. Brainstorm times when students might receive praise.

4. Make a general list of statements that could be used to give praise to a piece of writing. See Figure 1.1, Praise Statements, for ideas.

5. Post the list in the classroom to refer to during celebration. If students cannot come up with praise statements for a student's writing, the teacher should model some.

## Figure 1.1. Praise Statements

1. I like the title of your story.

2. I like the way you stuck to the topic of the piece.

3. Your characters' names are interesting.

4. Your adjectives describe the setting very clearly.

5. Your piece is in logical order and easy to follow.

6. I like the way you used figurative language.

7. Your story makes me laugh.

8. I like the topic of your piece.

9. Your beginning makes me want to hear more.

10. Your ending lets me know that the story is finished.

11. Your verbs describe a lot of action in the story.

12. Your story shows a lot of imagination.

13. Your story made me cry.

### Introducing the Question Technique
### for Celebration

1. Brainstorm with the class a list of possible questions that might be asked about a piece of writing. If students have difficulty coming up with questions, the teacher should model some for the class. See Figure 1.2, Model Questions, for ideas.

2. Post the list in the classroom for students to refer to when they are asking questions during celebration time.

3. Every piece of writing may not evoke questions. Therefore, you may skip this part during celebration and go right to the polish suggestions.

## Figure 1.2. Model Questions

1. Where did you get the idea for your piece?

2. How did you think of the title?

3. Are you finished with the piece?

4. What did you mean by _____ ?

5. Why did you write _____ ?

6. Where does your story take place?

7. Did you mean to say _____ ?

8. Is this a true story?

9. What will happen to your main character in the end?

10. Why didn't you _____ ?

11. Are you going to _____ ?

12. Are you satisfied with the story?

13. How many chapters are you going to make?

### Introducing the Polish Technique
### for Celebration

1. Have students name items that can be polished (e.g., cars, furniture). Discuss the benefits of polishing something.

2. Make a list of statements that could be used to improve (polish) a piece of writing. Stress the use of the word "could" instead of "should," because it is always the writer's choice to change something in his or her writing. If the students cannot think of statements, the teacher should model some. Refer to Figure 1.3, Model Polish Statements, for ideas.

3. Post the list in the classroom for reference during celebration.

## Figure 1.3. Model Polish Statements

1. You could change the title to make it fit better.

2. You could add more details.

3. You could take out the sentence that says _____ .

4. You could tell more about the character.

5. You could give more information about the setting.

6. You could separate this piece into two stories.

7. You could make the mystery scarier.

8. You could put the events of the story in a better order to make more sense.

9. You could use the pronouns in the place of nouns to avoid repetition.

10. You could take out the part where _____ .

11. You could move the first paragraph to the end.

12. You could start the story with dialogue.

## Setting Up Writing Folders

1. Choose some kind of permanent folder or portfolio in which students can house their writing in the classroom. I do not let these folders go home until the end of each semester. I send home a letter with an explanation and a request for participation by the parents. See Figure 1.4, Model Letter to Parents for Folders.

2. Discuss with the students how the folders will be used, what they will put in them, where the folders will be stored in the classroom, and how they will be passed out during writing time.

Figure 1.4. Model Letter to Parents for Folders

Dear Parents,

Your child has been learning to write through a process called writer's workshop. Each workshop session is divided into three parts: the minilesson, writing time, and celebration. During the minilesson, the teacher presents a writing lesson to the entire group. Following the lesson, students write about topics of their own choice from topic lists or other prewriting activities led by the teacher. At celebration time, a few students are chosen to read their pieces of writing out loud to the group in order to get feedback to improve the piece of writing. The students use a technique called PQP (praise, question, polish) to give the writer feedback in an organized way.

We are now at the end of the first semester of the year. I would like you to do three things with your child concerning writer's workshop. First, I would like you to look over your child's folder and let him or her explain the contents to you. Second, I would like your child to choose one piece of writing in the folder to share with you, using the PQP technique. Help your child edit the piece for mistakes in spelling, punctuation, and content. Third, have your child make a final copy of the piece that was chosen and return it to school with the folder. I hope that you have enjoyed sharing your child's writing.

Sincerely,
Mrs. Boone

I have participated in writer's workshop with my child.
Parent's signature _____
Date _____

## Introducing the Stages
## of the Writing Process

1. Have students interview a partner. Tell them that this is called "prewriting"—gathering ideas for writing.

2. Have each partner write a paragraph about the other from the interview notes. Tell them this is "drafting"—writing down ideas.

3. Have partners switch papers to check the accuracy of the information. Tell them this is "revising"—changing ideas only.

4. Have partners check each other's paper for errors in spelling, punctuation, capitals. Tell them this is "editing." Have them make a final copy. Label each of the four stages of the writing process on a sentence strip and post them in the classroom.

## Setting Up a Writing Area

1. Gather writing supplies and establish a writing area in the classroom. Include paper, pens, markers, paste, pencils, stapler, rubber stamps for the four stages of writing, some dictionaries, a thesaurus, and other materials you feel are necessary for writing.

2. Discuss with the class how this area is to be kept and whose responsibility it will be to clean it up.

3. Make visuals for the workshop such as a bulletin board, PQP signs, and a celebration sign. You might create a visual for each minilesson you do on the craft of writing and post it in the classroom for future reference.

### Making a PQP Response Form

1. After each student has read his or her piece during celebration time, choose a student or the teacher to fill out a PQP response form for the author. See Figure 1.5, Model PQP Response Form. It is only necessary to have questions written on the form that would lead to revising. Even though praise is given first, it is not necessary to record it. Give the form to the author to use during revision of his or her writing.

2. Share the form with the class and discuss how it will be used during writer's workshop.

## Figure 1.5. Model PQP Response Form

Date _____

Author's name _____

Title of writing _____

Questions asked:

1. _____

2. _____

3. _____

4. _____

5. _____

Polish suggestions:

1. _____

2. _____

3. _____

4. _____

5. _____

## Making an Editing Checklist

1. Decide which mechanical skills of writing are appropriate for your grade level. When students are ready to edit their writing, introduce a checklist for them to use. See Figure 1.6, Model Editing Checklist.

2. Make several copies and have them on hand in your writing center.

3. Discuss with students how and when to use the checklist.

## Figure 1.6. Model Editing Checklist

Date _____

Student's Name _____

Title of writing _____

____ I have checked for spelling.

____ I have checked for end punctuation.

____ I have checked for capital letters.

____ I have checked for complete sentences.

____ I have checked for verbs in sentences.

____ I have made new paragraphs for each topic.

____ I have put a name and date on the writing.

## Making a Spelling Chart

1. When students are writing their first draft, they should not be worried about spelling. Brainstorm a list of things they can do when faced with a word they cannot spell during the drafting stage. See Figure 1.7, Model Spelling Chart.

2. Continue the list to include how to find out the correct spelling of a word when they are editing their work. Encourage them to find ways other than asking the teacher to spell for them.

3. Post the list in the classroom, perhaps on a bulletin board, for future reference.

## Figure 1.7. Model Spelling Chart

### Spelling During Drafting

1. Invent a spelling.
2. Write the first two letters of the word and draw a line for the rest of the word.
3. Draw a picture or symbol for the word.
4. Write the first letter of the word and circle it.

### Spelling During Editing

1. Look in a dictionary or thesaurus.
2. Use a Franklin speller or other mechanical speller.
3. Use a word list.
4. Look in a book in the classroom.
5. Look around the classroom at posters, etc.
6. Ask another student.
7. Ask another adult.
8. Use the spell check on the computer.

## Purposes for Sharing During Celebration

1. When students read their writing during celebration, ask them to tell why they want to share their writing. The reason for sharing should be to improve the writing or move it forward in some way. Focusing students' attention on a specific purpose for sharing will give direction to their revisions.

2. Brainstorm with the class different reasons why writers would want to have others listen to their writing. If students cannot think of reasons, the teacher can model some. See Figure 1.8, Model Purposes for Sharing Writing.

3. Post the list of reasons for future reference.

## Figure 1.8. Model Purposes for Sharing Writing

1. To try something new

2. To see if the writing is clear

3. To finish a piece of writing and share the ending

4. To see if the piece is interesting

5. To use the polish suggestions

6. To use something taught in the minilesson

7. To get ideas for a title

8. To add more details to the writing

9. To get ideas for characters' names

10. To see if the sequence of ideas is clear

11. To get ideas for a different ending

12. To see if the dialogue is realistic

13. To see if the author created a mood for the story

### Modeling Peer Conferences

1. Before allowing students to have peer conferences, model with another student in front of the class the expectations you have for doing the conferences. Include the length of the conferences, where they are to be held, and the content of the conferences. Include other rules you may want to establish.

2. The content of the conferences will depend on the reason that the writer wants to get peer response. The reasons will be similar to those for sharing during celebration time (see Figure 1.8, Model Purposes for Sharing Writing). Model conferences often.

## Yearly Planning

After I had used the workshop approach for a few years, it occurred to me that I was developing a pattern of minilessons every semester. As I began to plan for a new year, I looked back on the lessons of the previous year and from them developed an outline that could be used for yearly planning. See Figure 1.9, Writer's Workshop Outline. I felt that some kinds of minilessons should be repeated every semester such as topic choice, revising, and editing; others, such as procedural lessons, needed to be introduced once. Each semester included required compositions for my grade level that were mandated by my school district, lessons on mechanics and the craft of writing, and curriculum lessons. The last semester I tried to use a project that would combine many of the writing skills we had used throughout the year. Several years we made books. Teachers who care to use the outline for yearly planning for the workshop should feel free to rearrange the order of the lessons used each semester. The order is not important. You may even want to change the kinds of lessons used. The important thing is to have some kind of outline of skills for each semester. You probably will not be able to do this the first year until you see what skills you want to teach and have had some practice with the workshop approach. The structure changed slightly each year for me as I found out what worked and what did not, learned more about the writing process, and discovered new materials to use.

## Figure 1.9. Writer's Workshop Outline

### First Semester

I.  Procedural lessons for setting up the workshop
    A.  Introduce three components
    B.  Start a topic list
    C.  Introduce praise, question, polish

    D. Set up writing folders

    E. Introduce the stages of the writing process

    F. Set up a writing area in the classroom

    G. Devise a PQP response form

    H. Devise an editing checklist

    I. Make a spelling chart

    J. Discuss purposes for sharing during celebration

    K. Model peer conferences

  II. Minilessons on topic choice, revising, editing

 III. Required compositions (mandated by curriculum in school district)

 IV. Curriculum lessons on nouns and verbs

  V. Minilessons on the craft of writing

    A. Show, not tell

    B. Beginnings

    C. Endings

 VI. Lessons on mechanics

    A. End punctuation

    B. Capitals

    C. Run-on sentences

VII. Evaluation of semester

## Second Semester

  I. Review procedures for the workshop

 II. Minilessons on topic choice, revising, editing

III. Required compositions

IV. Curriculum lessons on adjectives

 V. Minilessons on the craft of writing

    A. Expanding the topic

    B. Focusing the topic

    C. Using conversation

VI. Lessons on mechanics
    A. Capitals in titles
    B. Using commas, colons, semicolons
VII. Evaluation of the semester

## Third Semester

  I. Review procedures for the workshop
  II. Minilessons on topic choice, revising, editing
  III. Required compositions
  IV. Curriculum lessons on nouns, verbs, adjectives
  V. Minilessons on the craft of writing
    A. Figurative language
    B. Point of view
    C. Developing characters
  VI. Lessons on mechanics
    A. Combining sentences
    B. Quotation marks
  VII. Evaluation of the semester

## Fourth Semester

  I. Minilessons on topic choice, revising, editing
  II. Required compositions
  III. Curriculum lessons on adverbs
  IV. Minilessons on the craft of writing
    A. Looking at the way authors begin and end stories
    B. Using descriptive words to create mood
  V. Kinds of writing: informative, persuasive, imaginative
  VI. Making books

# 2

Topic-Choice Minilessons

Teachers need to introduce topic-choice lessons not only at the beginning of the year, but at regular intervals throughout the year. I use at least one topic-choice lesson at the beginning of each semester. Students need to be rejuvenated periodically to give them new ideas to write about. As each new topic is introduced, students add these ideas to their ongoing topic lists. The goal I set for my students was to get at least 100 ideas on their topic lists by the end of the year. Literature is an excellent source of ideas for topic-choice lessons. I have used old basal texts, anthologies, and novels to introduce an idea that an author does well in a particular story. Easy-to-read books are especially valuable, even for upper-grade students, because the entire book can be read in 10 to 15 minutes, which is the average length of a minilesson. The point in using these types of books is not the reading level of the book, but the ideas that the author conveys to the reader that are examples of good writing. Another excellent source for topic-choice minilessons is the book *If You're Trying to Teach Kids to Write . . . You've Gotta Have This Book* (1995) by Marjorie Frank. She describes finding topics to write about as "romancing" the students (Frank, 1995). See Stories to Use for Topic-Choice Minilessons in the Bibliography, p. 120.

## Making Webs

1. Have students make three circles on their papers. Label the circles "people," "places," "interests."

2. Give students time to web ideas for each circle. These ideas should pertain to their own lives.

3. Allow time to share ideas.

4. Have students begin a topic list from the web. Each item on the web is a separate topic. Use webbing often during the year.

5. Other possible categories for the web are sports, colors, pets, holidays, TV shows, movies, music, vacations, relatives, presents, dreams, friends, birthdays, and historical figures.

## Making Word Splashes

1. A word splash is created by splashing words at random on a page. Create a word splash for yourself. The words tell all about you. See Figure 2.1, Mrs. Boone's Word Splash.

2. Make a transparency of the word splash to share with the students.

3. Have students create their own word splashes.

4. Each word in the splash becomes a topic for students to add to their topic list.

5. Word splashes can be used in other subject areas to review vocabulary or concepts.

## Figure 2.1. Mrs. Boone's Word Splash

| | | |
|---|---|---|
| Kitty litter | Oldsmobile | Townhouse |
| (I have a cat) | (My new car) | (My house) |
| | | |
| Dancing | Writing | Reading |
| (A hobby) | (I enjoy it) | (I enjoy it) |
| | | |
| Peach | Calligraphy | Crunchy snacks |
| (Favorite color) | (A hobby) | (Favorite snacks) |
| | | |
| Southwest U.S.A. | Coach | Sister Act |
| (My last vacation) | (Favorite TV show) | (Favorite movie) |
| | | |
| February | Dolls | Samantha |
| (Birthday) | (A hobby) | (My cat's name) |

### Using Music

1. Play music for students to listen to in order to create a mood for writing. Instrumentals are best. I used the *Theme from the Pink Panther* and *Baby Elephant Walk* by Henry Mancini.

2. Have students draw pictures as they listen to the music.

3. Have students write from their drawings.

4. Use this idea several times a year.

5. Play background music as students write. My students enjoyed this minilesson very much.

## Using Literature #1

1. Read the story *The Relatives Came* (1985) by Cynthia Rylant to the class.

2. Have students tell about times when their relatives have visited them. Have them web these ideas.

3. Have students add these ideas to their topic list.

4. During writing time, the students can write stories about their relatives' visits.

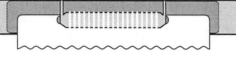

## Using Literature #2

1. Read the story *Charlie Anderson* (1990) by Barbara Abercrombie to the class.

2. The story has different categories that can be focused on: pets, cats, divorce, having two families. Choose one category to focus on.

3. Have students web ideas for the focus you chose.

4. Have students add these ideas to their topic list.

5. During writing time, have the students write about their ideas.

## Using Literature #3

1. Read the book *Alexander and the Terrible, Horrible, No Good, Very Bad Day* (1977) by Judith Viorst to the class.

2. Have students tell about a day they have had that is similar to Alexander's.

3. Have students add these ideas to their topic list.

4. During writing time, have the students write about their ideas. (My students were creative and came up with variations on this theme: "My Worst Vacation," "My Best Birthday," "My Worst Holiday").

## Using Literature #4

1. Read the story *Dear Brother* (1992) by Frank Asch and Vladimir Vagin to the class.

2. The story has different categories that can be focused on: letter writing, brotherly love, family, old things. Choose one category to focus on.

3. Have students web ideas for the focus you chose.

4. Have students add ideas to their topic list.

5. During writing time, have students write about their ideas.

## Using Literature #5

1. Discuss the characteristics of a good friend.

2. Read the story *Best of Friends* (1982) by Kerry Argent (Grades K-2) to the class.

3. Discuss the friendship in the story.

4. Have students make a list of people that they would consider to be their best friends, along with the characteristics that make them their best friends.

5. Have students add these names to their topic list.

6. During writing time, have the students write about these ideas.

## Using Literature #6

1. Ask students if they have ever done something that got them into trouble. Make a list of those experiences. Ask them if they ever jumped on their bed and got into trouble for it.

2. Read the story *No Jumping on the Bed* (1987) by Tedd Arnold to the class.

3. Discuss the consequences of the behavior in the book.

4. Have students add the experiences from Step 1 to their topic list.

5. During writing time, have students write about their ideas.

## Using Literature #7

1. Read the book *All About You* (1991) by Catherine and Laurence Anholt (Grades K-2) to the class.

2. Have students web some of the many categories that are presented in the book. You may want to use these categories on more than one occasion.

3. Have the students add these ideas to their topic list.

4. During writing time, have the students write about their ideas.

5. This book is a good one to use at the beginning of the year to establish many topics for writing.

## Using Literature #8

1. Read the book *If You Give a Mouse a Cookie* (1985) by Laura Joffe Numeroff to the class.

2. Brainstorm with students other titles that could be written following the format of the title of this book. Examples might be: "If You Give a Student Homework," "If You Give Me a Million Dollars," "If You Give a Teenager the Car."

3. Have the students add these ideas to their topic list.

4. During writing time, students can write about these ideas. Numeroff's book is also good for sequencing.

### Using Literature #9

1. Ask students to recall their first day of school.

2. Read the book *It Happens to Everyone* (1990) by Bernice Myers to the class. Using a Venn diagram, have the students compare Michael's first day of school with the teacher's.

3. Using the idea of first times, have students web topics for their topic list.

4. During writing time, have the students write about these ideas.

## Using Literature #10

1. Have students discuss going to their grandparents' house. Ask them if they think their grandparents have unusual or different things in their house. Name them.

2. Read the story *The Weird Things in Nanna's House* (1991) by Ann Maree Mason and Cathy Wilcox to the class.

3. Discuss the weird things in Nanna's house. Students may vote on whether they think the things are weird.

4. Have students add the ideas from Step 1 to their topic lists or make up a category called weird things and from that list add more topics.

5. During writing time, have students write about these ideas.

## Using Literature #11

1. Ask students if they have ever thought that their parents were weird. List things that the parents might have done that students thought were weird.

2. Read the book *Weird Parents* (1990) by Audrey Wood to the class. Compare the things that the boy's parents did that he thought were weird to the list made by the class.

3. Have students add these ideas to their topic list.

4. During writing time, have students write about their ideas.

5. The topic could be expanded to other weird things.

### Using Literature #12

1. Ask students to discuss if they have ever been sent to their rooms as punishment. Make a list of behaviors for which they were sent to their rooms. Also discuss what things they did in their rooms while there.

2. Read the book *Now Everybody Really Hates Me* (1993) by Jane Read Martin and Patricia Marx to the class.

3. Compare the girl's behavior in the book to the students' behavior.

4. Have students add these ideas to their topic list.

5. During writing time, have students write about these ideas.

## Using Literature #13

1. Have students web their favorite animals.

2. Read the book *I Love Animals* (1994) by Flora McDonnell to the class (Grades K-2). Have students add animals from the story to their webs.

3. Have students add the names of the animals to their topic list.

4. During writing time, have students write about the animals.

5. This book is also good for introducing verbs, or the discussion could be expanded to talk about pets.

## Using Food #1

1. Have students bring in their favorite snacks or provide a class snack.

2. Have students describe their snacks using the five senses. You may want to set up a matrix chart with the senses so that students can write a word to describe their snack under each sense.

3. Have students add these ideas to their topic list.

4. During writing time, have students write about their snacks.

## Using Food #2

1. Have students bring in a small amount of a dry cereal. In small groups, have students compare the cereals according to their shape, color, and taste. You might want to create a chart for them to record their responses.

2. Use the cereal as a motivator for possible fiction and nonfiction pieces (for example, reports on nutrition for each cereal).

3. Have students add these ideas to their topic list and write about them.

4. Other foods that would lend themselves to this lesson: crackers, cookies, fruit, cheeses, vegetables.

## Using Food #3

1. Have students bring a bottle or a container of their favorite soda or fruit juice. In small groups, let the students sample a variety of each.

2. Use the beverages as a motivator to write fiction or nonfiction pieces (for example, a letter to a company).

3. Have students add these ideas to their topic list.

4. During writing time, have students write about their ideas.

## Using Food #4

1. Have students bring in their favorite candy bars.

2. In small groups, have them compare the candy bars according to size, shape, taste, and ingredients.

3. Have the class make a list of all of their favorite kinds of candy bars (you could make a graph of them).

4. Brainstorm stories that have candy in them or are about candy (*Charlie and the Chocolate Factory*, *Chocolate Fever*, *The Chocolate Touch*).

5. Have students add these ideas to their topic list.

6. During writing time, have students write about candy.

### Using Food #5

1. Have students bring in raisins, or provide them for the class.

2. In small groups, have them brainstorm a list of some uses for a raisin other than for food. Have them share their lists with the class.

3. Use the raisins as a motivator to have students write fiction or nonfiction pieces (for example, a letter to a company telling it of their new use for the raisin).

4. Have students add these ideas to their topic list.

5. During writing time, have students write about raisins.

## Using Food #6

1. Have students bring in different kinds of pasta: shells, linguine, penne, fettuccine, spaghetti, macaroni.

2. In small groups, have students compare the pasta according to shape and size.

3. Use the pasta as a motivator for fiction or nonfiction pieces of writing during writing time. (Look at the shape of each kind and write a story that reminds you of the shape, for example, shells-seashore).

4. Have students add these ideas to their topic list.

### Using Feelings

1. Make a web of four circles labeled "scary things," "happy things," "silly things," and "things to be proud of." Complete the web for yourself. From one of the four circles, write a paragraph that tells about the words in that circle. Make a transparency of the web to share with the class.

2. Have students complete a web like the one above.

3. From one of the four circles, have them write about the ideas in a paragraph.

4. Have students add these ideas to their topic list.

5. You can use other feelings in later minilessons.

### Making Extended Webs

1. Brainstorm with the class broad topics that they are interested in, such as sports, hobbies, movies, and so on. Place one broad topic in the middle of an extended web (see Figure 2.2, Extended Webbing Model). Break down the broad topic into smaller ones to place in the extended parts of the web.

2. As a class, create a fiction or nonfiction piece of writing from the extended web.

3. Have students create an extended web for themselves.

4. Have students add these ideas to their topic list.

5. During writing time, have students write about ideas.

## Figure 2.2. Extended Webbing Model

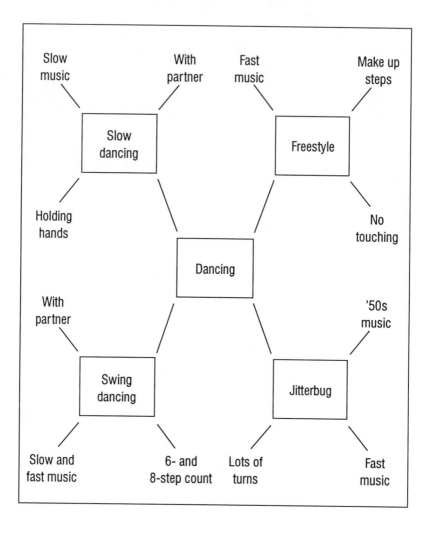

## Extended Brainstorming

Students often web for topics but do not fully explore them. Therefore, much of their writing lacks depth. A good technique to use to get students to expand their topics is called extended brainstorming. That is a term I made up, but it seems to fit the description given by Donald Murray (1990) in his book *Write to Learn* (pp. 31-36). You must first think of a topic that you really want to explore. Then begin to write down everything that comes into your head about the topic. Do not worry about how it comes out, just put it down as it makes itself known to you. Once you have exhausted the topic completely, then begin to look at what you wrote. Murray suggests looking for things that surprise you in your list. Circle them. Maybe a piece of writing will emerge from one of those surprises. Next, he suggests looking for connections among items on your list. Draw arrows to connect those items. Another piece of writing may emerge from those connections. See Figure 2.3, Extended Brainstorming Model, as an example of extended brainstorming.

Figure 2.3. Extended Brainstorming Model

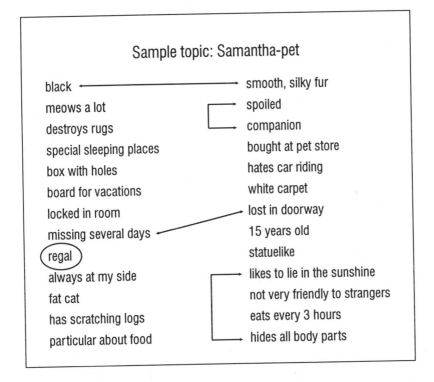

## Using Extended Brainstorming

1. Model extended brainstorming for students.

2. Have them try the technique.

3. Have students add these ideas to their topic list.

4. During writing time, have them write about their ideas.

## *Free Writing*

Free writing is writing continuously for a set period of time, say 10 to 15 minutes. During free writing, judgment is suspended, allowing ideas to flow. You may start with a topic or let one emerge. I gave students a topic in the beginning and then later announced that it was free writing time and they could write about any topic. Encourage students to keep the pencil to the paper until you call time. Sometimes this will mean writing something as mundane as "I'm stuck and have nothing to write about."

Free writing can be used to help students search for topics to write about, develop fluency, and collect ideas about a specific topic. It can be used across the curriculum to evaluate knowledge about content areas such as social studies or science. See Figure 2.4, Starters for Free Writing, for ideas. Try to think of new starters or have students think of some.

## Using Free Writing

1. Assign a sentence starter to begin free writing. You may want to begin with writing for 5 minutes and then extend the time to 10 or 15 minutes, depending on your students.

2. Students may want to share their writing at this time or wait until they have a complete piece of writing.

3. Have students add these ideas to their topic list.

## Figure 2.4. Starters for Free Writing

1. The best summer vacation would be . . .

2. The funniest thing that ever happened to me was . . .

3. If I had $100 I would . . .

4. Some days I feel like . . .

5. I'm glad that . . .

6. I love to . . .

7. I can never remember to . . .

8. I really get angry when . . .

9. The scariest thing that ever happened to me was . . .

10. If I could go anywhere in the world I would go to . . .

11. My favorite season is . . .

12. I will never get used to . . .

13. The best job in the world would be . . .

14. I wish my family would . . .

15. My favorite color is . . .

Remember to keep writing until time is called.

# 3

# The Craft of Writing: Minilessons

How do you teach someone to write? Donald Murray (1990) says, "There is no *way* to write" (p. 39, emphasis added). Thank heaven! I have been looking for the "correct" way to teach students to write for 25 years. Actually, when I worked on my undergraduate degree in teaching, there were no courses on teaching writing to children. I approached the subject the same way that I was taught to write: assigning students a topic, grading the completed assignment, and returning the assignment with maybe a few comments and a letter grade.

The teaching of writing has improved greatly in recent years. Writing is now recognized as a recursive process, moving back and forth between stages as the writer composes. Students are no longer stuck with topics assigned by the teacher. Teachers are using topic choice in workshop settings to give students more freedom to tap into subjects that interest them. Students get the opportunity to work on a piece of writing more than one time if they use the process approach to writing.

When I began to use writer's workshop in my classroom, one of the most difficult tasks I faced was deciding what I should teach students about writing. I used the scope and sequence of skills that was mandated by my school district, but I still needed to find minilessons on the craft of writing. These were at first time consuming and difficult to create. That is why I wanted to include a section in this book on the craft of writing.

As I began to develop lessons on my own, I was still frustrated with some of the writing I was getting from my students. Even though I gave them lessons on plot, character, and setting, their stories still seemed to lack a focus or had a problem that needed to be solved. I began to reread some of the experts in the field of teaching fiction writing.

Lucy Calkins (1986) devotes a chapter to the teaching of fiction in her book *The Art of Teaching Writing.* I highly recommend that all teachers of writing read it to get a better understanding of how to teach students the essentials of fiction. Donald Graves (1989) has written a book specifically dealing with that topic called *The Reading/Writing Teacher's Companion: Experiment With Fiction.* Graves's information is invaluable as well. Gail E. Tompkins (1990) discusses narrative writing in Chapter 4 of her book *Teaching Writing: Balancing Process and Product.* She includes 11 charts on story concepts and what each story concept includes. These charts are very useful to teachers for introducing the elements of narrative writing to students.

Nancie Atwell (1987) lists seven keys to writing good fiction in her book *Writing, Reading, and Learning With Adolescents: In the Middle.* In summarized form, they are as follows:

1. Write what you know.

2. Create and stay with one main character.

3. Describe your main character's thoughts and feelings.

4. Spin a believable plot.

5. Establish a narrative voice.

6. Develop a theme.

7. Apply all of the elements of effective personal experience narratives to writing fiction: specific information, context (who, what, where, when, why), description, dialogue, action, motivation, graceful language, a "grabbing" lead, and a satisfying conclusion. (Atwell, 1987, p. 139)

I must add a caution from Calkins's book. She says that we cannot just pile a bunch of techniques onto students and expect that their writing will improve. They need to know about plot, characters, setting, theme, and mood. Those essential parts of a story should be taught in reading classes as well as writing classes. However, these elements are meaningless unless students have a vested interest in their writing. What Calkins suggests is that students write fiction from their own experiences, from ideas and topics that have meaning for them. Isn't this the basis for the writer's workshop approach to teaching writing? Calkins (1986) says, "The story should mean something, reveal something that matters. Only when the story matters to the writer will it matter to the reader. Write from a topic that burns. Choose a topic that is so important that you can feel it in your body" (Calkins, 1986, p. 322).

Instead of piling techniques onto students, we can help them improve their writing with minilessons that can be interwoven into their writing. Students will acquire a "bag of tricks" for writing that can be stored in their folders and brought out when a particular tool is needed. Teaching fiction with this approach will be challenging, yet rewarding.

The minilessons in this chapter are about teaching students the craft of fiction writing. They are a collection of techniques that can be added to the writer's "bag of tricks." Some of these ideas can be considered revision techniques rather than beginning techniques. If you wish to use them in this way, that's okay. Also, sometimes it can be easier to teach a technique after students have written a story, rather than before. The first lessons establish word banks for students to use as they write. Later lessons give students techniques for writing stories. An essential part of these lessons is looking at the literature that already exists so that students can see how established writers approach a topic and looking at student's own writing as examples of what to do and what not to do. The students' writing provides a starting point to work from.

### Building Word Banks: Verbs

1. Read the book *Kites Sail High* (1988) by Ruth Heller to the class.

2. Define *verb*. Have students list verbs that were mentioned in the book.

3. In small groups, have students make a list of verbs. Each group can list different kinds: *-ing*, *-ed*, irregular, base form. Have students share lists with the class.

4. Make copies of the lists to give to students to keep in their writing folders for reference.

5. Teachers may want to expand this lesson to include other verb lessons.

### Building Word Banks: Adjectives

1. Read the book *Many Luscious Lollipops* (1989) by Ruth Heller to the class.

2. Define *adjective.* Have students list the adjectives that were mentioned in the book.

3. In small groups, have students make a list of adjectives. Share the lists with the class.

4. Make copies of the lists to give to students to keep in their writing folders for reference.

5. Teachers may want to expand this lesson to include other adjective lessons.

## Building Word Banks: Nouns

1. Read the book *A Cache of Jewels and Other Collective Nouns* (1987) by Ruth Heller to the class.

2. Define *noun.* Have students list the nouns that were mentioned in the book.

3. Divide the class into small groups. Assign each group a category from which to develop a list of nouns: school, home, pets, movie stars (make up your own categories if you like).

4. Have students share the lists with the class.

5. Make copies of the lists to give to students to keep in their folders for reference.

6. Teachers may want to expand this lesson to include other noun lessons.

## Building Word Banks: Adverbs

1. Divide the class into small groups. Assign each group one of the following questions: How? Where? When? Why? and To what degree or extent? Have them make a list of words that answer their question.

2. Have students share the lists with the class. The teacher should eliminate words that are not adverbs. Tell the class that these words are called adverbs. Define *adverb*.

3. Make copies of the lists for students to keep in their writing folders for reference during writing time.

4. Teachers may want to expand this lesson to include other adverb lessons.

## Looking at Parts of Speech in Literature

1. Find an excerpt from a basal reader or other piece of literature that uses strong or vivid nouns, verbs, adjectives, or adverbs.

2. Make a transparency or read the excerpt to the class.

3. Have students identify examples of the particular part of speech you want them to notice from the excerpt.

4. Discuss how these words affect the writing.

5. Do a separate minilesson for each part of speech.

## Looking at Parts of Speech in Students' Writing

1. Immediately following the minilesson on looking at parts of speech in literature, do the following lesson.

2. Have students choose a piece of their own writing. Have them look at how they used the part of speech that you focused on in the previous lesson.

3. If students have examples that are worthwhile, ask them to share the examples with the class. If students need to improve their use of a particular word, have them rewrite those sentences. Have them share the "before" and "after" pieces. Have the class decide if the changes are effective.

## Creating Class Stories

1. Teachers may want to create several class stories before letting students create their own. This can be done in a minilesson, or you can step outside of the workshop approach and do a longer lesson. If you use the minilesson, you may have to do it in several segments. You could do one story element in each minilesson.

2. Donald Graves (1989) describes an excellent method for creating class stories in his book *The Reading/Writing Teacher's Companion: Experiment with Fiction* (pp. 28-32). See Figure 3.1, Creating Class Stories, for more details.

## Figure 3.1. Creating Class Stories

Donald Graves (1989) leads the first session in creating class stories; then he has the children do later ones. He starts by having the class choose a problem to be solved. As he moves through the story, he continually restates the information that they suggest. After they have given a general plot, he moves on to the characters, working on their names, appearance, and behaviors. Next, he brings in setting. Last, he works on the starting plot action and how the plot unfolds to reveal the characters. He plays a guiding role as he continually questions, summarizes, challenges, and points out inconsistencies in the information that the students suggest. The students vote on the elements that are incorporated into the story. Graves varies the story element that begins each class story.

Using this process will give students lots of practice in setting up stories before they do it on their own. I highly recommend this method.

## Showing, Not Telling

1. Make a transparency of the sentences in Figure 3.2, Showing Versus Tellling. Discuss the difference between the two types. Ask which type of writing is more effective (showing).

2. Give students one sentence at a time from Figure 3.3, Topics for Showing, Not Telling. Have them write a paragraph showing the idea instead of telling it. Share the paragraphs with the class.

3. After introducing this lesson to the class, give them sentences to show instead of tell for their journal exercises in the morning. I found this practice helps improve students' writing.

## Figure 3.2. Showing Versus Telling

| Telling | Showing |
| --- | --- |
| 1. I was really hot. | 1. Sweat dripped off of my glasses. The dry T-shirt that I put on this morning stuck to my body. Everything I touched was sopping wet. |
| 2. Daren's voice sounded funny. | 2. Daren's voice echoed and boomed as if he were talking into a megaphone. |
| 3. They enjoyed the movie. | 3. As they left the theater, they were laughing so hard they could hardly talk. "I'd see that again tomorrow, wouldn't you?" Marie managed to gasp. |
| 4. She was sad when her cat died. | 4. She cried every day for a week. Whenever she looked at the place where Caramel slept, she thought of all the fun they had playing together. |

## Figure 3.3. Topics for Showing, Not Telling

1. It was a cold day.

2. The cat was scared.

3. Mr. Johnson was poor.

4. The house was a mess.

5. The party was fun.

6. Janie looked happy.

7. Our vacation was a disaster.

8. The car was getting old.

9. There were lots of people in the streets.

10. The little girl was afraid.

11. The circus clown was tall.

12. My room looks like a cyclone hit it.

13. The newborn kitten was tiny.

14. The assignment was difficult.

15. The ice cream melted in the car.

### Identifying Story Elements

1. Give students lots of practice identifying setting, characters, plot, problems, and solutions in literature.

2. Read stories appropriate for your students. Use the Graphic Organizer (Story Map) in Figure 3.4 to identify story elements.

3. After practicing with story elements in literature, introduce each element into the writer's workshop. There is no specific order for introducing them.

4. By this time, students should have many pieces of writing of their own to refer to. Use their writing as examples for revision to improve their story elements.

## Figure 3.4. Graphic Organizer (Story Map)

TITLE _____

SETTING _____

CHARACTERS _____

_____

PROBLEM _____

_____

EVENTS _____

1. _____

2. _____

3. _____

4. _____

5. _____

SOLUTION _____

_____

_____

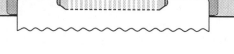

### Reading and Writing: Beginnings, Middles, and Endings

1. Read stories that are appropriate for your students.

2. Have students fold a plain piece of paper into three sections. Label the sections beginning, middle, and end. Younger students may draw a picture to illustrate each part of the story. Older students can write sentences to retell each part of the story in the appropriate section.

3. Give students lots of practice with this type of lesson before having them write their own stories.

4. Have students create their own stories using this technique.

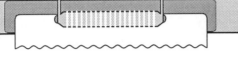

## Creating Story Problems and Solutions

1. Brainstorm with students schoolwide problems: noisy hallways, lack of playground facilities, no paper towels in bathrooms—whatever is appropriate for your school.

2. Choose one of the problems as the basis for a story. As a class or in small groups, have students write a story that includes the problem and creates a solution for it.

3. In a separate minilesson, have students brainstorm problems in their own lives. Use the same technique for creating individual stories.

4. Have students share stories and judge them for effectiveness.

## Finding a Focus for Stories

1. After students have been writing for a while, you may see stories without a focus or that contain a list of unrelated events or ideas. See Figure 3.5, Sample Unfocused Story.

2. The best source for examples of unfocused stories is your classroom. Find a piece of such writing and ask the student's permission to use it. Make a transparency of it.

3. Guide students with questions such as What is the main idea of this story? Eliminate sentences that do not relate to the main idea. Rewrite the story. This is a revision technique. Do this minilesson several times.

## Figure 3.5. Sample Unfocused Story

My Brother

My brother is very active. He likes the Power Rangers. When I have a friend over he is very nice. He is smart. He has Ms. Salni for first grade. He said she is very nice. When he was in kindergarten he had Mrs.Williams. He said that she was the nicest teacher he had. My brother is six. His name is Billy. Billy has five fish and I have three fish. I have a gerbil that he plays with all the time. Billy loves my gerbil. My brother hates homework. He had about 15 Power Ranger cards but he gave me five cards. A lot of my friends think he is cute. I don't care what anybody says I will always love him.

## Looking at Leads for Stories

1. Read to students or have them read several excerpts from stories that have different leads.

2. Make a list of different ways authors begin stories (description, conversation, narration). Discuss the effectiveness of each way. Students should keep this list in their writing folders or post it in the classroom for reference.

3. Have students look at leads in their own writing. They may experiment with creating different leads for stories.

4. See Bibliography, Stories to Use for Leads, p. 121.

## Looking at Endings for Stories

1. Read to students or have them read several excerpts of story endings. Discuss the different ways authors end the stories. Focus on the tone set by the final line of the story.

2. Have students look at endings in their own writing. They may experiment with creating different endings for the stories.

3. Have students share the stories with the class, reading the old and new endings. The class can judge for effectiveness. This is a revision technique.

4. See Bibliography, Stories to Use for Endings, p. 122.

## Writing Paragraphs

1. To reinforce the idea of writing in paragraphs, assign a topic that has a specific number in it, such as two birthday presents you received. See Figure 3.6, Student Samples: Writing Paragraphs.

2. Have students share the paragraphs. Discuss topic sentences and supporting details with the class.

3. Sample topics: two of your best friends, three places you have visited, three favorite holidays, two favorite subjects, three people you admire, two hobbies or interests, three favorite animals, two worst days.

## Figure 3.6. Student Samples: Writing Paragraphs

### Sample #1

I got very many presents for Christmas. My very favorite was Orlando, Florida. My family and I are going to Orlando, Florida on February 9th and coming home on February 17th. The way I found out was I saw this paper in my stocking. I said to my brother Ryan, there's something in our stockings. We went to see what is was. All of the sudden my brother yells "We're going to Orlando Florida. I can't wait."

Another present I got was a kareoke machine. It is a tape player that comes with two microphones and if you put special tapes in the words come up on the T. V. I am very happy about all my presents. I know I have a family that cares about me.

### Sample #2

One of the gifts I got for Christmas was a Mary Poppins doll. It was very cool. The umbrellas that Mary floated with came with it, and the beak moved up and down.

Another present I got was the Genie from Aladdin. The Genie came with all his clothes in the movie, including the outfit when the Genie was freed. He even had the goofy hat. I like all my gifts, but these were my favorites.

## Looking at Settings for Stories

1. Read several stories that have specific settings to students. See Bibliography, Stories With Specific Settings, p. 122.

2. Have younger students draw the setting after having heard the story. Have older students tell what the setting is and how important it is to the story. Ask the question, Would the story be different if the setting was changed? Discuss the technique the author used to create the setting of the story.

3. In separate minilessons, have the students look at settings in their stories and judge them for effectiveness.

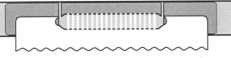

## Looking at Point of View in Literature

1. In several minilessons, read examples of stories written from different points of view to students. See Bibliography, Stories to Use for Point of View (p. 123), for ideas.

2. Discuss with students from whose point of view the story is written. How does the character's point of view affect the story? How would the story be different if told from another character's point of view?

3. Different versions of familiar fairy tales would be good examples of stories told from different points of view. See Figure 4-16 in Gail E. Tompkins's book, *Teaching Writing: Balancing Process and Product* (1990) for ideas.

## Writing Stories From Different Points of View

1. Choose an event or part of a familiar story for students to rewrite from a different point of view. (Example: rewrite *Snow White and the Seven Dwarfs* from one of the dwarfs' points of view). Younger students may be capable of telling the story orally rather than writing it.

2. Have students share stories and evaluate the effectiveness of the changes.

3. When you feel students are ready, have them look at point of view in their own writing. Younger students may not be capable of doing this. Revise as necessary.

## Looking at Character Names

1. Have students name a memorable character from a piece of fiction they have read: Charlotte, Wilbur, Aunt Spiker, Aunt Sponge, Mrs. Basil E. Frankweiler, Ramona, Beezus, Rumpelstiltskin, Cinderella, and so on.

2. Web the personality traits of the characters. See if there is a relationship between the names of the characters and their personality traits.

3. Have students share their webs. Students with similar characters can compare their webs.

4. Guide students in choosing character names in their writing.

## Looking at Character Traits

1. Have students read a piece of fiction from their own writing while the rest of the class makes a list of the character traits of one character that are revealed in the piece.

2. Guide students in a discussion to see if enough character traits were revealed to paint a clear picture of the character for the reader.

3. Use this discussion as a basis for revision for writing.

4. Do this lesson for more than one character and repeat it often throughout the year.

## Looking at Characters in Literature

1. Read excerpts from several stories that describe or give the reader a good picture of one of the characters. See Bibliography, Stories to Use for Developing Characters (p. 124), for suggestions.

2. Discuss how the author lets the reader know about the character (e.g., actions, feelings, description, dialogue).

3. Make a list of ways to develop characters. Have students keep the list in their writing folders for reference during writing.

4. Do this lesson several times throughout the year.

5. Have students look at how they have developed characters in their own writing.

### Creating Characters

1. Using some type of art medium, have students make an animal or human character.

2. Have students write a story about their characters.

3. Have students use a checklist (see Figure 3.7, Checklist for Character Development) to evaluate the characters in the story.

4. Have students share their stories with the class in order to evaluate character development. The class may refer to the Checklist for Character Development (Figure 3.7) for criteria.

5. This minilesson will take more than one session to develop. Divide it wherever appropriate for your class.

## Figure 3.7. Checklist for Character Development

Character's Name _____

1. My character is realistic.                           Yes ___ No ___

2. I have described my character's appearance.    Yes ___ No ___

3. I have shown how my character acts.             Yes ___ No ___

4. I have shown how my character feels.            Yes ___ No ___

After looking at the checklist, I will make the following changes in my
character: _____

_____

_____

_____

_____

_____

_____

_____

## Looking at Dialogue in Literature

1. Read several examples of stories that use dialogue to the class.

2. Have students discuss the effectiveness of dialogue. Discuss the purpose of using dialogue in a story. Have students make a list and keep for reference when writing.

3. In a separate minilesson, have students look at the punctuation used in writing dialogue.

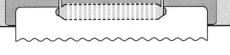

## Writing Dialogue

1. Find a cartoon to make into a transparency, whiting out the existing dialogue, or use pictures of people that could inspire dialogue.

2. As a class, have students write dialogue. Show them how to indent and use correct punctuation for each new speaker.

3. Have students work in pairs to create dialogue from motivational activities that you provide.

4. Have students look at dialogue that they have written in their stories or give them the chance to try some.

5. This lesson should be done in several sessions.

## Qualifying Dialogue

1. Have students examine dialogue in stories appropriate for your grade level.

2. Make a class list of verbs that are used to qualify the dialogue such as *said, whispered,* and *cried.*

3. Brainstorm verbs that could be used to replace the word *said* in a sentence. Make a list and give students a copy of the list to keep in their folders for reference during writing time. See Figure 3.8, Words to Qualify Dialogue, for ideas.

4. Have students look at dialogue already written in their own stories. Replace the verb *said* with verbs from the list created in Step 3.

## Figure 3.8.  Words to Qualify Dialogue

| | | |
|---|---|---|
| added | admitted | advised |
| agreed | announced | answered |
| argued | asked | barked |
| begged | blurted | boasted |
| bragged | commanded | complained |
| continued | cried | declared |
| demanded | directed | echoed |
| encouraged | exclaimed | gasped |
| giggled | groaned | growled |
| hesitated | hollered | insisted |
| instructed | interrupted | invited |
| joked | laughed | moaned |
| mumbled | muttered | objected |
| ordered | pleaded | remarked |
| repeated | replied | roared |
| screamed | shrieked | sighed |

### Expanding Sentences

1. On the chalkboard or overhead, write a simple sentence that can be expanded. See Figure 3.9, Ideas for Expanding Sentences, for examples.

2. Have students give suggestions for expanding the sentence with adjectives, adverbs, or phrases.

3. Compare the sentences for effectiveness before and after adding words. Give students practice using several examples.

4. Have students look at ways of expanding sentences in their own writing. Repeat this lesson often during the year.

## Figure 3.9. Ideas for Expanding Sentences

1. My friend enjoys math.

2. Reading is fun.

3. The shark chased me.

4. Bring me a sandwich.

5. The television isn't working.

6. Lunch is ready.

7. My cat is fat.

8. The snow melted.

9. Mr. Black is a friendly man.

10. The mirror got broken.

11. The coat was torn.

12. Our house is big.

13. The street curved.

14. California is a coastal state.

15. Deliver the mail.

16. Wait for me.

## Creating Descriptive Writing #1

1. To give students practice observing people and events, take them to a place inside or outside of the school (e.g., cafeteria, gym, another classroom, playground).

2. Have them record their observations.

3. Return to the classroom and have students share descriptions. Discuss the details used in the descriptions. These observations could be topics for future writing.

4. Repeat this lesson throughout the year. Observation is an excellent way to learn descriptive writing.

## Creating Descriptive Writing #2

1. On the weekend or over a holiday, give students a homework assignment to write a description of an event that occurred at that time. You may want to limit the length of the assignment, depending on the grade level and ability of your class.

2. When students return to school, have them share their descriptions with the class or a partner. Discuss accuracy of details and vividness of descriptions.

3. Students may want to rewrite their descriptions to improve them. If so, share the revisions as well.

### Looking at Figurative Language

1. In several minilessons, read examples of stories that use figurative language to the class. See Bibliography, Stories That Use Figurative Language (p. 124), for ideas.

2. For older students, identify the type of figurative language used in the story.

3. Have students try to write figurative language that follows the pattern of the type used in the stories you share with the class.

4. Have students share pieces of their previous writing that used figurative language or try to incorporate it into those pieces if possible.

5. Make a list of the kinds of figurative language and post the list in the classroom.

## Choosing Titles for Stories

1. Display several familiar books.

2. Guide a discussion about the titles of the books. Discuss things such as the title's length and appropriateness and capitalization of words in the title.

3. In other minilessons, read a story to the class without revealing the title. Have students brainstorm possible titles for the story.

4. Have students read their own stories out loud. Let the class evaluate the effectiveness of the title.

5. Students may use celebration time to have the class suggest titles for stories the author is having trouble choosing a title for.

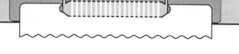

## Considering Audience in Writing

1. Have students brainstorm people for whom they might write something. Include the type of writing that they would use (e.g., a letter to friend, a Christmas list to parents, or a diary for oneself). Post the list in the classroom for reference.

2. Discuss how writing for different people might be different.

3. To have students experience the effect of style on audience, in other minilessons have them write a diary entry for themselves about some event that has occurred. Then have them take the same event and write a letter to their parents telling about it. Compare the styles.

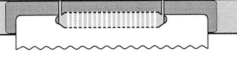

### Considering Different Genres in Writing

1. In small groups, have students make a list of different kinds of writing. See Figure 3.10, Kinds of Writing, for ideas.

2. Have students share the lists with the class.

3. Make copies for students to keep in their folders for reference during writing time.

4. Do minilessons on some of the different kinds of writing, especially those that are required for your grade level.

## Figure 3.10.  Kinds of Writing

| | |
|---|---|
| Personal experience narratives | Biographies |
| Autobiographies | Essays |
| Reports | News stories |
| Jokes and riddles | Advertisements |
| Poems | Acrostics |
| Diaries | Plays |
| Recipes | Interviews |
| Lists | Slogans |
| Contests | Letters |
| Invitations | Forms |
| Fictional narratives | Fairy tales |
| Children's books | Speeches |
| Editorials | Songs |
| Scrapbooks | Fables |
| Commercials | Advice columns |
| News reports | Cartoons |

## Combining Sentences

1. In order to give students practice combining sentences, use Figure 3.11, Sentences for Combining, or make up your own.

2. Give them other exercises similar to this one for further practice throughout the year.

3. Have students examine sentences in their own writing to see if they can be combined.

4. Have them share their revisions with the class and evaluate them for effectiveness.

## Figure 3.11. Sentences for Combining

1. Cats are fluffy and warm.    Cats have soft fur.

2. Oranges are juicy.    Oranges are good for you.    Oranges have vitamin C.

3. Mr. Jones is tall.    Mr. Jones is thin.    Mr. Jones has a beard.

4. The ball is round.    The ball is red.

5. Maryland is near the mountains.    Maryland is near the ocean.

6. I like ice cream.    I like cake.

7. A bird has wings.    A bird has feathers.    A bird has a beak.

8. The elephant is a large animal.    The elephant has a trunk.

9. Jack's car was painted.    Jack's car was red.

10. A whale swims in the ocean.    A whale is a mammal.    A whale is large.

11. Our school bought new computers.    Our school bought printers.

12. Pick up candy at the store for me.    Pick up fruit at the store for me.

13. He waited a long time for us to come home.    He waited until 6 o'clock.

14. A tiger is a fierce animal.    It stalks its prey.

15. Phillip has a dog.    Phillip has a cat.    Phillip has a gerbil.

# Appendixes:
# Forms for the Workshop

## Using Forms

I devised several different forms to evaluate writer's workshop, keep track of conferences, summarize each semester's work, and give the students tips on what to look for in the following semester.

Appendix A is the form I used at the end of the first semester of the school year to evaluate students' progress in the workshop and help me assess students for a language arts grade. Individual pieces of writing were never graded. Students' language arts grades were a combination of work done in all writing, including journals, writer's workshop, and writing in the content areas. Near the end of the semester, each student filled out a conference sheet and brought it with him or her to the conference along with his or her writing folder. The conferences took the place of minilessons for a week, but we still had writing time and celebration each session of the workshop.

I used the form in Appendix B for the second and third semesters of the year. This form is different to reflect changes in the students' writing. Individual conferences were held, following the same format as in the first semester.

Appendix C is the form I used to evaluate the workshop for the entire school year. This was a good tool for students to use, as it enabled them to see their progress throughout the year in writing.

Appendix D was used to keep track of daily individual conferences that I had while the students were writing. This was a good monitoring device for grading, for parent conferences, and for ideas for minilessons. Appendix E is a sample conference sheet.

Appendixes F and G are copies of transparencies I used at the end of the second and third semesters to review what we had done in the workshop and give students tips for the next semester.

## Appendix A: Evaluation Conference—First Semester

Name _____ Date _____

Answer the questions below. Be ready to discuss them at the
conference. Bring your writing folder.

1. What does someone have to do to become a good writer? _____

   _____

2. What is the most important thing you learned about writing this
   semester? _____

   _____

3. What is your best piece of writing this semester? _____

   _____

   Why? _____

   _____

4. Do you use the four stages of writing? _____

   _____

5. Have you participated in responding to other's writing during
   celebration time? _____

   _____

6. Have you used the suggestions given to you during celebration
   time? _____

   _____

7. What are your writing goals for next semester? _____

   _____

## Appendix B: Evaluation Conference—
## Second and Third Semesters

Name _____ Date _____

1. Has your writing changed since the first semester?   Yes__ No__

2. Are you using the different stages of writing?        Yes__ No__

3. Do you volunteer to read your writing?                Yes__ No__

4. Are you using the polish suggestions?                 Yes__ No__

5. Are you on task during writing time?                  Yes__ No__

6. Are you using any ideas from the minilessons?         Yes__ No__

7. What do you like about your writing? _____

   _____

   _____

   _____

8. What don't you like about your writing? _____

   _____

   _____

   _____

9. What are your writing goals for next semester? _____

   _____

   _____

   _____

## *Appendix C: Yearly Evaluation*

Name _____ Date _____

1. What things did you learn about writing this year that you didn't know before? _____

2. How do you usually get ideas for writing? _____

_____

3. How long does it take you to write a first draft? _____

_____

4. Do you revise?____ What do your revisions consist of? _____

_____

5. Do you find mistakes when you edit a piece? _____

_____

6. What kind of mistakes do you find most often? _____

_____

7. Did you respond with someone this year? _____

_____

8. Did the response help to make the writing better? _____

_____

9. Has your writing changed in any way this year? _____

If so, explain. _____

10. What was your best piece of writing this year? _____

_____

11. What made it your best? _____

_____

## Appendix D: Individual Conference Record

Teacher's conference record for _____

| Date and Title of Piece | Skills Used Correctly | Skills Needed to Be Taught |
| --- | --- | --- |
| | | |

## *Appendix E: Sample Individual Conference Record*

Teacher's conference record for _____

| Date and Title of Piece | Skills Used Correctly | Skills Needed to Be Taught |
|---|---|---|
| 9/25 School | Complete sentences Sequencing ideas Concluding sentence Commas in a series | Paragraphing |
| 10/23 Pizza | Writing about one topic | Making the topic more interesting |
| 11/7 The Night Before Christmas | Writing about a personal experience | Paragraphing for each new speaker |
| 11/21 The Lion, the Witch, and the Wardrobe | Many details to tell a summary | Using main ideas only |
| 1/7 May | Can write a poem | Write about one topic |
| 1/8 The Lion, the Witch, and the Wardrobe | Followed directions for revisions | None |

## Appendix F: Summary and Tips for Second Semester

1. Summary of evaluations: What does a person have to do to become a good writer? Discuss with the class.

2. Add to your 100-topic list.

3. Required this semester: two more compositions, including one that has gone through all stages of the writing process.

4. Don't forget prewriting.

5  Edit in different colors. Attach editing sheet to piece for editing folder.

6. Check the need and time for peer conferences.

7. Keep movement in the room to a minimum.

8. Stay on task.

9. Write on every other line. Do not write on the back of your draft copy.

10. Make a list of ways to improve writing.

11. What makes good writing?

12. Use revision techniques.

## *Appendix G: Tips and Reminders for Third Semester*

### THIRD SEMESTER

Two more required pieces

One piece that has gone through all stages to go into class notebook

### *REMEMBER!*

Date all pieces.

Use the stages of writing.

Use the suggestions given at celebration time or conference time.

Do a variety of pieces.

Stay on task.

Skip lines on rough draft.

Attach editing sheet to final copy.

# Bibliography

## Books on How to Write

Atwell, N. (1987). *Writing, reading, and learning with adolescents: In the middle.* Portsmouth, NH: Heinemann.

Calkins, L. (1986). *The art of teaching writing.* Portsmouth, NH: Heinemann.

Fletcher, R. (1993). *What a writer needs.* Portsmouth, NH: Heinemann.

Frank, M. (1995). *If you're trying to teach kids to write . . . You've gotta have this book.* Nashville, TN: Incentive.

Graves, D. (1989). *The reading/writing teacher's companion: Experiment with fiction.* Portsmouth, NH: Heinemann.

Graves, D. (1991). *The reading/writing teacher's companion: Build a literate classroom.* Portsmouth, NH: Heinemann.

Murray, D. (1990). *Write to learn.* Fort Worth, TX: Holt, Rinehart & Winston.

Tompkins, G. E. (1990). *Teaching writing: Balancing process and product.* Columbus, OH: Merrill.


## Other Sources on Writing and Teaching Writing

Brown, D., & Burnette, B. (1987). *Criteria for writers.* New York: Holt, Rinehart & Winston.

Carratello, J., & Carratello, P. (1993a). *Write all about it: 1, 2, 3-TCM-500.* Huntington, CA: Teacher Created Materials.

Carratello, J., & Carratello, P. (1993b). *Write all about it: 3, 4, 5-TCM-501.* Huntington, CA: Teacher Created Materials.

Carratello, J., & Carratello, P. (1993c). *Write all about it: 4, 5, 6-TCM-502.* Huntington, CA: Teacher Created Materials.

Carratello, J., & Carratello, P. (1993d). *Write all about it: 6, 7, 8-TCM-503.* Huntington, CA: Teacher Created Materials.

Graves, D. (1989). *Investigate nonfiction.* Portsmouth, NH: Heinemann.

Olson, C. B. (Ed.). (1987). *Practical ideas for teaching writing as a process.* Irvine, CA: Bureau of Publications, California State Department of Education.

Zinsser, W. (1990). *On writing well* (4th ed.). New York: Harper.


## Music

Mancini, H. (1984). *Henry Mancini Collection* [record]. New York: RCA Records.


## Children's Literature

Abercrombie, B. (1990). *Charlie Anderson.* New York: Macmillan.

Anholt, C., & Anholt, L. (1991). *All about you.* New York: Penguin.

Argent, K. (1988). *Best of friends.* Boston: Little, Brown.

Arnold, T. (1987). *No jumping on the bed.* New York: Dial.

Asch, F., and Vagin, V. (1992). *Dear brother.* New York: Scholastic.

Martin, J. R., & Marx, P. (1993). *Now everybody really hates me.* New York: HarperCollins.

Mason, A. M., & Wilcox, C. (1991). *The weird things in Nanna's house.* New York: Orchard.

McDonnell, F. (1994). *I love animals.* Cambridge, MA: Candlewick.

Myers, B. (1990). *It happens to everyone.* New York: Lothrop.

Numeroff, L. J. (1985). *If you give a mouse a cookie.* New York: HarperCollins.

Rylant, C. (1985). *The relatives came.* New York: Macmillan.

Wood, A. (1990). *Weird parents.* New York: Dial.

## Stories to Use for Topic-Choice Minilessons

Alexander, M. (1989). *My outrageous friend Charlie.* New York: Dial.
   *Topics: friendship, story twist, believing in yourself*

Aliki. (1982). *We are best friends.* New York: Greenwillow.
   *Topic: friendship*

Allard, H. (1985). *Miss Nelson has a field day.* Boston: Houghton Mifflin.
   *Topic: surprise ending*

Jensen, V. (1977). *Sara and the door.* Reading, MA: Addison-Wesley.
   *Topic: memories*

McPhail, D. (1979). *Where can an elephant hide?* New York: Doubleday.

*Topic: story ending*

Medearis, A. (1990). *Picking peas for a penny.* Austin, TX: State House.

*Topic: biographical poem*

Merriam, E. (1991). *The wise woman and her secret.* New York: Simon & Schuster.

*Topic: teaches a lesson*

Zolotow, C. (1973). *Janey.* New York: Harper & Row.

*Topic: memories*

## Books to Use for Building Word Banks

Heller, R. (1987). *A cache of jewels and other collective nouns.* New York: Scholastic.

Heller, R. (1988). *Kites sail high.* New York: Scholastic.

Heller, R. (1989). *Many luscious lollipops.* New York: Scholastic.

## Stories to Use for Leads

Blos, J. (1987). *Old Henry.* New York: Morrow.

Burningham, J. (1985). *Granpa.* New York: Crown.

Conford, E. (1973). *Felicia the critic.* New York: Little.

Lionni, L. (1967). *Frederick.* New York: Pantheon.

Rylant, C. (1985). *The relatives came.* New York: Macmillan.

Steig, W. (1988). *Spinky sulks.* New York: Farrar, Straus & Giroux.

Yorinks, A. (1986). *Louis the fish.* New York: Farrar, Straus & Giroux.

## Stories to Use for Endings

Aliki. (1979). *The two of them.* New York: Greenwillow.

Asch, F. (1984). *Just like Daddy.* New York: Simon & Schuster.

Bunting, E. (1989). *The Wednesday surprise.* St. Louis, MO: Clarion.

Dupasquier, P. (1988). *Dear Daddy.* New York: Puffin.

McKissack, P. (1986). *Flossie and the fox.* New York: Dial.

Polacco, P. (1993). *The keeping quilt.* Columbus, OH: Read Advent.

Van Allsburg, C. (1988). *Two bad ants.* Boston: Houghton Mifflin.

Wood, A. (1991). *King Bidgood's in the bathtub.* San Diego, CA: Harcourt Brace.

Yorinks, A. (1986). *Louis the fish.* New York: Farrar, Straus & Giroux.

## Stories With Specific Settings

Anderson, H. C. (1979). *The ugly duckling.* New York: Harcourt Brace.

Babbitt, N. (1975). *Tuck everlasting.* New York: Farrar, Straus & Giroux.

Baker, J. (1988). *Where the forest meets the sea.* New York: Greenwillow.

Browne, A. (1990). *The tunnel.* New York: Random House.

Cauley, L. B. (1984). *The town mouse and the country mouse.* New York: Putnam.

Ekoomiak, N. (1992). *Arctic memories.* New York: Henry Holt.

George, J. C. (1972). *Julie of the wolves.* New York: Harper & Row.

George, W. T. (1989). *Box turtle at long pond.* New York: Greenwillow.

Hartley, D. (1986). *Up north in winter.* New York: Dutton.

Konisburg, E. L. (1983). *From the mixed-up files of Mrs. Basil E. Frankweiler.* New York: Atheneum.

MacLachlan, P. (1985). *Sarah, plain and tall.* New York: HarperCollins.

McCloskey, R. (1969). *Make way for ducklings.* New York: Viking.

Oram, H. (1985). *In the attic.* New York: Henry Holt.

White, E. B. (1952). *Charlotte's web.* New York: Harper & Row.

## Stories to Use for Point of View

Blos, J. (1987). *Old Henry.* New York: Morrow.

Brown, M. (1954). *Cinderella.* New York: Scribner.

Cleary, B. (1981). *Ramona Quimby, age 8.* New York: Random House.

George, J. C. (1972). *Julie of the wolves.* New York: Harper & Row.

Grahame, K. (1961). *The wind in the willows.* New York: Scribner.

Lionni, L. (1969). *Alexander and the wind-up mouse.* New York: Pantheon.

Lobel, A. (1972). *Frog and toad together.* New York: Harper & Row.

Lowry, L. (1979). *Anastasia Krupnik.* Boston: Houghton Mifflin.

McNulty, F. (1986). *The lady and the spider.* New York: HarperCollins.

Scieszka, J. (1989). *The true story of the three little pigs.* New York: Viking.

Van Allsburg, C. (1988). *Two bad ants.* Boston: Houghton Mifflin.

Viorst, J. (1977). *Alexander and the terrible, horrible, no good, very bad day.* New York: Atheneum.

Yashima, T. (1976). *Crowboy.* New York: Puffin.

## Stories to Use for Developing Characters

Ackerman, K. (1988). *The song and dance man.* New York: Knopf.

Aliki. (1979). *The two of them.* New York: Greenwillow.

Babbitt, N. (1975). *Tuck everlasting.* New York: Farrar, Straus & Giroux.

Burningham, J. (1985). *Granpa.* New York: Crown.

Cleary, B. (1983). *Dear Mr. Henshaw.* New York: Morrow. (Most of Cleary's books
    are appropriate.)

Cohen, B. (1983). *Molly's Pilgrim.* New York: Lothrop.

Cooney, B. (1992). *Miss Rumphius.* New York: Viking.

Fitzhugh, L. (1964). *Harriet the spy.* New York: Harper & Row.

Hewett, J. (1987). *Rosalie.* New York: Lothrop.

Howe, D., & Howe, J. (1979). *Bunnicula.* New York: Atheneum.

Lowry, L. (1979). *Anastasia Krupnik.* Boston: Houghton Mifflin.

Parish, P. (1970). *Amelia Bedelia.* New York: Scholastic.

Paterson, K. (1978). *The great Gilly Hopkins.* New York: Corwell.

Spinelli, J. (1993). *Maniac Magee.* Thorndike, ME: Thorndike.

Yorinks, A. (1986). *Hey, Al.* New York: Farrar, Straus & Giroux.

## Stories That Use Figurative Language

*Alliteration*

Ahlberg, J., & Ahlberg, A. (1978). *Each peach pear plum.* New York: Penguin.

Aylesworth, J. (1994). *My son John.* New York: Henry Holt.

Blos, J. (1987). *Old Henry.* New York: Morrow.

## Onomatopoeia

Wood, A. (1988). *Elbert's bad word.* New York: Harcourt Brace.

Yolen, J. (1987). *Owl moon.* New York: Philomel.

## Repetition

Ackerman, K. (1990). *The banshee.* New York: Philomel.

Albert, B. (1991). *Where does the trail lead?* New York: Simon & Schuster.

Arnold, T. (1988). *Ollie forgot.* New York: Dial.

Aylesworth, J. (1994). *My son John.* New York: Henry Holt.

Mason, A., & Wilcox, C. (1991). *The weird things in Nanna's house.* New York: Orchard.

Medearis, A. (1991). *Dancing with the Indians.* New York: Holiday House.

## Rhyme

Ahlberg, J., & Ahlberg, A. (1978). *Each peach pear plum.* New York: Penguin.

Arnold, T. (1988). *Ollie forgot.* New York: Dial.

Aylesworth, J. (1994). *My son John.* New York: Henry Holt.

Medearis, A. (1990). *Picking peas for a penny.* Austin, TX: State House.

Medearis, A. (1991). *Dancing with the Indians.* New York: Holiday House.

Morgenstern, C. (1991). *Good night feet.* New York: Henry Holt.

## Similes

Ackerman, K. (1990). *The banshee.* New York: Philomel.

Yolen, J. (1987). *Owl moon.* New York: Philomel.

## Strong Verbs

Cherry, L. (1990). *The great kapok tree.* New York: Harcourt Brace.

Simon, N. (1971). *I know what I like.* Morton Grove, IL: Albert Whitman.